# Prairie Explorer

**Mary Quigley**

Chicago, Illinois

Editorial: Marta Segal Block/Jennifer Huston
Photo research: Bill Broyles
Production: Sal d'Amico
Map: Guy Holt
Printed and bound in China by Wing King Tong

09 08 07 06 05
10 9 8 7 6 5 4 3 2 1

**Library of Congress Cataloging-in-Publication Data:**
Quigley, Mary, 1963-
  Prairie explorer / Mary Quigley.
    p. cm. -- (Habitat explorer)
Includes bibliographical references (p.   ).
Contents: Prairie roots -- Prairie dog village -- Bison --
Today's tall grasses.
  ISBN 1-4109-0513-6 (lib. bdg. : hardcover)
  1-4109-0841-0 (paperback)
  1.  Prairie ecology--Great Plains--Juvenile literature. 2.
Great  Plains--Juvenile literature. [1. Prairie ecology. 2.
Ecology. 3. Great Plains.] I. Title. II. Series.
  QH104.5.G73Q55 2004
  577.4'4'0978--dc22
                                2003017124

**Acknowledgments**
The publisher would like to thank the following
for permission to reproduce photographs:
Title page, pp. 9, 16, 22 Corbis; icon, pp. 4, 19 Robert
Lifson/Heinemann Library; pp. 6, 14 Stephen J.
Krasemann/DRK Photo; pp. 7, 26, 27 D.
Cavagnaro/DRK Photo; pp. 8, 25 Joe McDonald/DRK
Photo; p. 10 Layne Kennedy/Corbis; p. 11 Bob
Gurr/DRK Photo; p. 12 Marty Cordano/DRK Photo; p.
13 Michael Ederegger/DRK Photo; pp. 15, 18
PhotoDisc/Getty Images; pp. 17, 23 Wayne Lynch/DRK
Photo; p. 20 William Campbell/DRK Photo; p. 21 The
University of Nebraska-Lincoln School of Natural
Resources; p. 24 Jeff Daly/Visuals Unlimited; p. 28
Lynn M. Stone/DRK Photo; p. 29 Craig Aurness/Corbis

Cover photograph by Corbis

# Contents

Any words appearing in the main text in bold, **like this,** are explained in the glossary.

# The Great Prairie

You are on a flat plain in the summer. The day is hot but a light breeze makes it comfortable. You have entered the Great Prairie. This prairie stretches from Wyoming in the west to Chicago in the east and from Canada in the north down to Texas in the south. Many grasses grow here, but few trees. You hear a meadowlark singing overhead. With so few trees to perch on, many birds sing

## Explorer's notes

The Great Prairie goes through parts of Canada and these U.S. states:

Colorado, Illinois, Kansas, Montana, Missouri, Nebraska, New Mexico, North Dakota, Oklahoma, South Dakota, Texas, Wyoming

**Many plants and animals are at home in the prairie.**

while flying. Many miles east there are more trees, taller grasses, and many wildflowers. This is because there is more rainfall in that part of the prairie.

## Prairie habitats

Many animals live on the Great Prairie. This is their **habitat.** A habitat is a place where plants and animals live.

**There are temperate grasslands throughout the world. In the United States these habitats are known as prairies.**

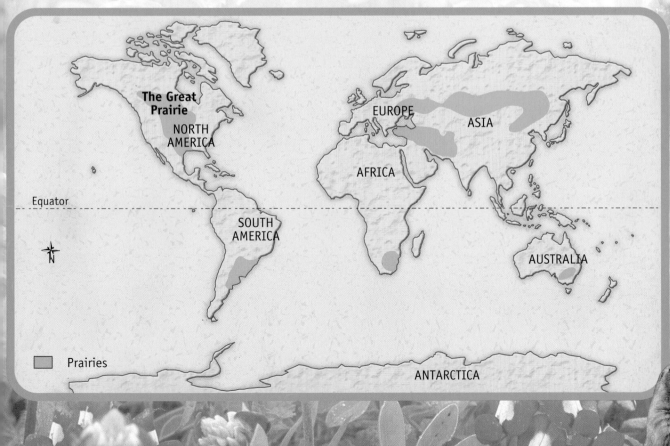

The Great Prairie

NORTH AMERICA

EUROPE

ASIA

AFRICA

Equator

SOUTH AMERICA

AUSTRALIA

N

Prairies

ANTARCTICA

# Prairie Grass

There is a lot of grass on the prairie. This is because most grasses do not need much rain to grow. Even if lightning starts a fire and burns everything to the ground, the grass can still grow back. The roots are protected under the ground. Grass can also survive cold winters and snow by being **dormant.**

## Deer snacks

Trees grow from the tips. Grazing animals, like deer and buffalo, nibble them down. They do not grow back. Grass grows from the roots, so after the animals have finished their meal, the grass starts growing again.

This means that the plant stops growing until things warm up. The thin blades bend in the strong winds that would damage other plants. Blades of grass point upward so only the very tips get scorched by the sun.

The grass improves its prairie home by weaving strong roots together into a sturdy support that holds the soil in place to prevent **erosion.** Erosion is when wind or water carves out the land.

These coneflowers and thistles add color to the prairie landscape.

## Explorer's notes

Some common prairie plants:
- bluestem
- coneflower
- arrowfeather
- weeping love grass
- blazing star
- black-eyed Susan
- thistle

# Prairie Homes

You have to look carefully to find some of the animals that live on the prairie. There are not a lot of places to hide, so many of the animals are very fast. This helps them get away from their **predators.** Predators are animals that eat other animals. **Prey** are the animals that are eaten.

## River visitors

Rivers can attract animals. Along the path of rivers are animal communities. When the rivers overflow, they create **marshes** where frogs and salamanders thrive.

Ground squirrels and other animals visit rivers for a quick drink.

These pronghorn antelope are on the lookout for danger.

## Burrows

Some prairie animals live in **burrows.** Burrows are underground homes that animals create by digging through the dirt. They can have many tunnels and separate rooms for sleeping, eating, and getting rid of body waste.

Explorer's notes

Some prairie animals:
- coyotes
- birds
- foxes
- buffalo
- deer
- antelope
- snakes
- salamanders
- prairie dogs

# Short-Grass Prairie

Not all of the Great Prairie is the same. You have begun your journey in the short-grass prairie. It is known as the Great Plains. It is the driest part. Short-grass prairie plants **adapt** to the shortage of water. Some are light colored. This helps them to reflect away the heat of the sun. Others have protective coatings such as wax or fuzz to hold in moisture and keep them cool.

## Prairie potholes

Even in the driest parts of the prairie there is some water. Dents made by glaciers many years ago are called prairie potholes. Rainwater collects in them. Plants grow at their edges. These areas draw a lot of animals and can be a favorite stopping place for migrating, or traveling, birds.

Most plants of the short-grass prairie are no more than 2 feet (1/2 meter) tall. There are few trees and the ones that do

**Prairie potholes hold water between rain showers.**

## Explorer's notes

Features of the
short-grass prairie:

- dry
- few trees
- plants are short

grow, such as willows and cottonwoods, grow next to streams.

Thorns and spikes are plant protection that makes it difficult for them to be eaten. Prairie winds that cause snowdrifts and **droughts** also help the plants **reproduce**. Wind helps pollinate plants. Pollination is when grains of pollen from one plant are deposited on another plant and a seed begins to form. The seeds may then be carried to a new place by the wind.

**This Canadian short-grass prairie is part of a national park.**

# Insects of the Prairie

A lot of insects make their home on the prairie. The dung beetle has a very messy job, rolling little balls of **manure** across the prairie in order to have a place to lay eggs. The newborn dung beetles eat the manure. Their lifestyle and eating habits make them an important part of the prairie's clean-up crew.

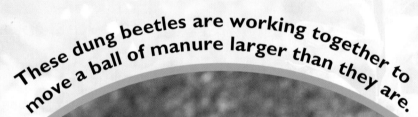

These dung beetles are working together to move a ball of manure larger than they are.

By moving and eating the manure, the dung beetles help to recycle and distribute the manure as **fertilizer** for prairie dirt. The prairie is full of other insects such as grasshoppers and dragonflies. At night you can hear the crickets.

## Explorer's notes

Some birds of the prairie:

- blue jays

- goldfinches

- oriole red-winged blackbirds

**Many birds survive by eating the insects that live in the prairie.**

# Prairie Dog Village

Ahead of you are mounds of earth with holes. Prairie dogs have worked hard to dig out a home in the dirt using long, sharp claws. A prairie dog does a back flip to signal danger, or makes a sound like a dog's bark. This barking is how prairie dogs got their name. Prairie dogs are actually rodents, related to squirrels and mice.

**Prairie dog burrows have many different tunnels.**

# Communities

Prairie dogs are very social. They like to live in large tunnel towns. They talk with each other by making sounds, touching each other, and movements like the back flip. Although prairie dogs have a lot of **predators** like coyotes, bobcats, badgers, and eagles, they have a wonderful defense system, too. They all work together to keep their community safe. Abandoned prairie dog **burrows** hide other animals.

*Prairie dogs got their name because they make a sound like a dog's bark.*

### Explorer's notes

Animals that live in old prairie dog burrows and tunnels:
- owls
- rabbits
- rattlesnakes

# Mixed-Grass Prairie

After traveling 250 miles (400 kilometers), the land changes. You are now in the mixed-grass prairie. Many plants are taller here. It is not as dry. There are more places for rattlesnakes to hide. While many of the plants are the same as in the short-grass prairie, there are some additional ones that would not grow well with less rain. Ducks are swimming in a nearby prairie pothole. There are a lot of ducks and potholes in the mixed-grass prairie.

**A rain storm is about to hit this mixed-grass prairie.**

# Eating and balance

**Predators** keep nature in balance. They eliminate animals that are weak from disease. This keeps disease from spreading. They keep populations stable. Predators only hunt for as much as they need to survive. Animals that eat plants also help keep things in balance by trimming back plants and helping to distribute seeds from the foods they eat. Animals that only eat meat are called **carnivores.** Animals that only eat plants are **herbivores** and those that eat both meat and plants are **omnivores.**

Snakes find plenty of places to hide in the mixed-grass prairie.

## Explorer's notes

Some mixed-grass prairie animals:
- antelope
- prairie dogs
- Swift foxes
- eastern cottontails
- earthworms
- box turtles
- ducks
- coyotes

# Butterflies

Many colorful butterflies skim the breeze around you. One lands on the brim of your hat. A monarch butterfly drinks from milkweed flowers. This is the only plant a monarch will lay eggs on. It is called a host plant. For most animals this plant is poisonous, but not for the monarch. When the caterpillars come out of their tiny eggs they will eat the leaves of the milkweed and become poisonous to **predators** such as birds.

## Grounded

If it is too hot or cold, butterflies cannot fly. In the heat of the day they rest on the cool edges of a muddy puddle.

**Adult monarch butterflies drink nectar from a variety of flowers.**

In a few months, thousands of monarchs will **migrate** as far as Central Mexico to avoid the cold prairie winter. You see a spicebush swallowtail caterpillar chewing on a leaf. This caterpillar has spots that look like big eyes. With a smooth green body and big eyes, this caterpillar could be mistaken for a small snake. Lantana and goldenrod flowers grow thick around you. Painted lady butterflies have waited for the temperature to be just right for flying.

**These colorful flowers are attractive to butterflies and other insects.**

# The Buffalo Roam

You have come to a **nature preserve.** Every plant and animal in this preserve is both protected and wild. A group of American bison, also called buffalo, are grazing. Their fur looks uncomfortable but they need it for the upcoming cold winter. In the dry summer, bison can go without water for days. One bison lowers his large body onto the ground and rubs his back in the dirt to get rid of insects.

## Explorer's notes

Bison **adaptations:**
- woolly coat
- can go without water for days
- uses herd for protection
- teeth designed for grazing and chewing plants
- rolls in dirt to get rid of insects

Bison are protective of the calves in their herd.

# Herds

Bison stick together in a herd for protection even though they are strong and are the largest, heaviest land animals in North America. They guard young calves in the middle of their circle. If they are frightened they **stampede,** running for miles. It sounds like thunder.

## Bison landscapers

Bison help their **habitat** by grazing and grooming the grasses. They like to walk while they graze so they trim a lot of prairie. Their hooves push seeds down into the ground where they can sprout.

**This preserve in Nebraska is home to many bison.**

# Tall-Grass Prairie

You have traveled 450 miles (724 kilometers) and arrived in the tall-grass prairie. You can smell wildflowers, grass, and dirt. Bees hover near clover where they gather the **nectar** that they will make into honey. Because it rains a lot here the soil is **fertile** and there are wide patches of farmland. Here some of the grasses are taller than you.

## Twisters

A tornado occurs when cold air meets hot air and begins to swirl, creating a funnel-shaped cloud. If the funnel cloud touches down, it can cause a lot of damage. Tornadoes are also known as cyclones or twisters.

**Warning signs of a tornado include a dark and greenish sky, hail, a wall cloud formation, and a roaring sound like a train.**

Prairie chickens live in the tall-grass prairie.

The compass plant has leaves that point north and south, like a compass, in case you get lost. There are a lot of butterfly milkweeds, blazing stars, sunflowers, coneflowers, and pasture roses. Moss, herbs, and flowers grow among the grasses. Prairie chickens dance and make loud noises to attract mates. Today the wind makes the tall grasses whisper, but sometimes weather churns into a tornado on the Great Prairie.

Explorer's notes

Three types of prairie:
- short-grass
- mixed-grass
- tall-grass

23

# Pocket Gophers

A furry animal hurries into a **burrow.** You might think that you have found another prairie dog village. But prairie dogs do not live in the tall-grass prairie. You have seen their cousin, the pocket gopher. Pocket gophers create burrows, much like a prairie dog's. Sometimes their burrows can be as long as 200 feet (60 meters) and have several rooms.

Fireflies create light because of a chemical reaction in their bodies. Their lights do not get hot.

Pocket gophers are named for their cheek pockets.

The pocket gopher has a special **adaptation** that keeps dirt out of its mouth when it is digging. It can close its lips behind its teeth. Evening brings fireflies, flashing in the tall grasses, and a glimpse of a coyote.

## Explorer's notes

Prairie dogs:
- social
- live in short- and mixed-grass prairie

Pocket gophers:
- like to be alone
- live in tall-grass prairie

# Farms on the Prairie

The tall-grass prairie has **fertile** soil that farmers like. Many of the tall grasses today are corn, wheat, and oats grown by farmers instead of big bluestem and squirreltail growing wild. The soil is rich because lots of **organic** material is a part of it. Things like decaying plants feed the dirt.

**Much of the food we eat is grown in farms on what used to be prairie land.**

This helps new plants to grow. The tall-grass prairie also has enough rain to keep the **crops** growing. A lot of food that people eat comes from farms on the prairie. Many farmers are trying to grow their crops while still protecting prairie **habitats.**

## New uses

Much of the original tall-grass prairie is now used for farming, industry, or living space.

# The Changing Prairie

Many **native** prairie plants and animals have been removed from their **habitat** by the building of cities and certain farming methods. Many prairie dogs, wolves, bears, and bison have been killed. Sometimes they were killed because they were feared and sometimes they were viewed as pests. Farm animals such as cattle have taken a lot of the grazing space. Plants and animals that are not native to the Great

## Explorer's notes

Threats to the Great Prairie:

- building of cities

- certain farming practices

- killing of prairie animals

**Cattle need a lot of prairie land on which to graze.**

Prairie have been brought here on purpose and by accident. Sometimes they take over the habitat of a native species.

## Saving prairies

Many people who love the prairie are bringing back the plants and animals that belong there so everyone can enjoy this beautiful area of land and sky. Parks and preserves are now home to many prairie plants and animals. Some animal populations are being increased through protection programs.

**This town in Iowa used to be a prairie habitat.**

# Find Out for Yourself

One of the best ways to learn about the prairie is to visit one. There are many places where prairies are being restored and preserved. Some of them are open to the public. There are also many people who are adding prairie plants to their own yards.

Explore the Internet to find out more about prairies. Websites can change, so if the links below no longer work, use a kid-friendly search engine, such as www.yahooligans.com or www.internet4kids.com. Type in keywords such as "prairie animals" or even better, the name of a particular animal.

## Websites

www.nwf.org
The National Wildlife Federation has information on prairie animals and how to help protect them.

www.nationalgeographic.com/kids/
This site created by National Geographic magazine contains games and information about prairies and the plants and animals that live there.

## Books to Read

Baldwin, Carol. Living in a Prairie. Chicago: Heinemann, 2003.

Butterfield, Moira. Animals on Plains and Prairies. Chicago: Raintree, 2000.

Woodward, John. The Secret World of Prairie Dogs. Chicago: Raintree, 2004.

# Glossary

**adapt/adaptation** change in response to habitat

**burrow** underground living space, or the act of making an underground living space

**carnivore** meat eater

**crop** plant grown for food

**dormant** at rest

**drought** time of very dry weather conditions

**erosion** wearing away land with wind or water

**fertile** good for growing plants and crops for food

**fertilizer** substance used to make soil better for growing

**habitat** place where a plant or animal lives

**herbivore** animal that eats only plants

**manure** bodily waste of an animal. Manure makes soil better for growing plants.

**marsh** soft, wet land with grasses and plants

**migrate** move from place to place in search of better conditions

**native** originating in a certain place

**nature preserve** habitat in which the plants and animals are protected by law and nature is undisturbed

**nectar** liquid made by plants that is the main ingredient in honey

**omnivore** animal that eats both meat and plants

**organic** natural, not treated with chemicals

**predator** animal that hunts other animals for food

**prey** animal that is hunted to be food

**reproduce** make another living thing of the same kind

**stampede** run quickly and wildly when frightened

# Index